More Magic Wo

Creating Figures and Pictures
with Dyed Wool

Angelika Wolk-Gerche

More Magic Wool

Creating Figures and Pictures
with Dyed Wool

Floris Books

Translated by Anna Cardwell
Photographs of Figures 7–9, 11–16, 35, 62 by Dieter Wolk,
Winterbach, all others by Wolpert & Strehle, Fotodesign,
Stuttgart.
Illustrations by Angelika Wolk-Gerche.

First published in German under the title
Märchenwolle by Verlag Freies Geistesleben
First published in English in 2001 by Floris Books

The Story of the Moss-Woman (p. 48) from Elisabeth Klein,
Von Zwergen und Gnomen, Novalis Verlag, Schaffhausen.
The poem (p. 58) is from *Peter William Butterblow,* by
C.J. Moore, Floris Books

British Library CIP Data available

ISBN 0-86315-351-8

Printed in Belgium

Contents

Introduction

Unspun natural sheep's wool with its light, fluffy nature and — when dyed — radiant colours, is no ordinary material, but a natural product imparting a sense of magic, as we have named it here.

For centuries and millennia, people have expressed their need for colour using natural materials to create subtle shades. However, with the use of chemical dyes, colours are brighter and harsher, and our sense of colour is assaulted and desensitized. The warm, harmonious colours offered by plant dyes give a different colour experience, comforting our eyes. Magic wool's fluffiness, suppleness and warmth is a delight for our sense of touch, increasingly inspiring teachers and therapists to use it.

This book gives instructions and inspiration for working with magic wool both for beginners and for people who already have experience in this area.

What is Magic Wool?

Magic wool is plant-dyed, teased or carded unspun sheep's wool. The raw wool should be high quality from healthy sheep and processed carefully. Dyeing is done slowly and with non-toxic mordants.

Magic wool is known mainly for the *wool pictures* that can be made out of it. The fibres of the wool stick to each other and onto a rough background like felt, resulting in a variety of effects. These pictures are full of life, light and colour, as dyed wool is affected by different light conditions. The ability of wool to be moulded into three-dimensional figures is surprising, the creative possibilities manifold.

Dolls made of this wool seem to glow from the inside, because the light is reflected against the different layers of coloured wool. The fact that both wool and plant dyes are derived from living processes surely lends more magic — a delight for heart and hands!

Magic Wool with Children

A kindergarten teacher once told me that in her experience, magic wool had a calming effect on the children, the room often became quiet while they were using it.

Another kindergarten teacher had the idea of letting the children colour their own wool: the children drew a thick layer of colour with wax crayons onto strong paper, and then rubbed and twisted their wool tufts onto it until they acquired an even colouring. They teased small birds out of these tufts and stuck two feathers in them for wings.

A tuft of coloured wool in half a walnut shell can be a decorative surround for a coloured stone. You can also hang the tufts on thin threads from a branch to create a simple mobile, or make a wool picture using a felt background.

Figure 1. Tufts of wool, coloured with wax crayons.

Figure 2. Mobile, tufts of wool on a branch.

9

Figure 3. Tufts of wool tied on a thread.

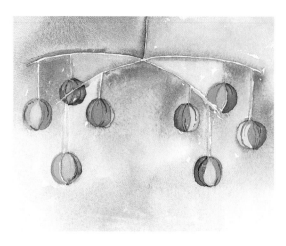

Fig. 4. Mobile out of wool balls (see p. 28).

Magic wool in the nursery

For babies and toddles tie together a bunch of rainbow coloured wool. Hung above the changing table, babies will look at it again and again. A mobile is more work, but small children love watching it and are stimulated by its movement. For toddlers keep to the simple primary colours (red, blue and yellow) or their pastel shades. A simple mobile can be created by fastening tufts of wool to a curved branch. Make sure the spacing does not allow the tufts to get tangled.

Place a basket with magic wool in the children's room for playing with. At first adults should still show them how to use the wool carefully, but children will pick up quickly how much can be done with it. It need not be something specific: young children will make beds and nests for their dolls and soft animals, as well as making landscapes with meadows, mountains, lakes and flowers on the floor. Pictures are easily made with tufts of wool laid onto a felt background. Older children can make simple figures or items like braided hair-bands.

Working with magic wool is espe-

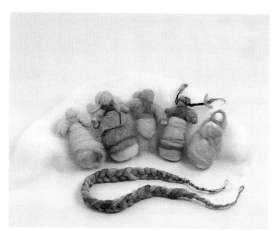

Figures 5 and 6. Simple things made by children.

cially beneficial for ill or convalescing children.

From time to time, sort the wool by colours, and tease or card it again to keep the fluffiness of the wool. Add a new colour every now and again. Wash the wool if necessary.

Figure 7. Woolly milk sheep with lambs.

Figure 8. This red-capped gnome is hardly bigger than a hand.

From sheep to gnomes

It can be a very special experience for children to see sheep being shorn, and then to be able to take some wool home. There they can enjoy sorting and teasing the wool. They can feel their hands becoming greasy and supple while the wool becomes cleaner and fluffier. While washing the wool they can watch the water becoming dirty and the wet wool becoming cleaner. After washing, the wool loses its pungent 'natural' odour and smells much sweeter.

The plants needed for dyeing can also be collected with children. Ideally, try to find them locally with the children.

Dyeing is particularly interesting, as the wool and plant dyes are brought together to create something new. Never leave the children alone with the hot dyeing pots in case they burn themselves. Impatient children can be told that the wool and dyes need some time to 'get to know each other and become friends,' helped by occasional stirring on your part.

After thorough rinsing and drying the wool is teased again to loosen it before carding. While teasing it is a good opportunity to tell stories, maybe about sheep. If the wool is intended for making gnomes, stories, rhymes and songs can be told to 'entice' the gnomes to come.

The finished colourful mass of wool is itself beautiful and inspiring. Children love its softness. It can be formed into a circle, for instance to surround a colourful fruit or a precious stone. It can be made into a figure, such as a gnome, but to increase the magic of these creatures, don't let young children help to make them.

The next chapter describes in detail how to make magic wool. It is also possible to buy magic wool if you want to start making things right away.

Figure 9. Girl with a freshly shorn fleece.

13

Making Magic Wool

Discovering 'new' colours

To begin with use plants which you can find locally. You will become more observant of the local environment and the passing seasons, and be able to build a personal range of colours.

Every climatic zone, every landscape in the world has its own colour language, and it is fun to discover those colours. In Europe, for instance, they are mainly yellow, yellow-orange, yellow-green, brown and shades of pink. At first this may seem a limited range, but with practice different shades can be made, and the eye begins to perceive subtleties of colour in the surroundings. Appreciating nature's colour harmonies can promote well-being in today's fast-moving garishly-coloured world.

Plant-dyed colours can be mixed and blended without clashing, unlike chemical colours. This is because the colours contain aspects of all other colours. The oldest colours of the world are naturally dyed ones, for instance in cave paintings. Archeologists have found textiles dyed from mignonette, indigo and cochineal, among other materials. The textiles are best preserved in dry climates such as in Egypt where materials from the Copts are still bright and shining today, or in Peru where the pre-Colombian Incas were masters of dyeing.

Figure 10. Colour circle.

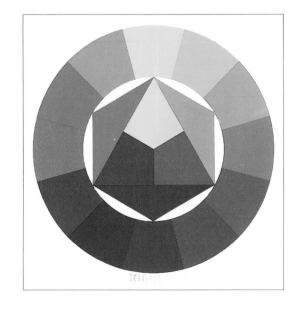

Collecting the plants

If you have a garden you can plant some dyeing plants in it — for instance, marigold, tagetes, camomile and spinach. Plant onions in early spring (their skins give colour), and grow sunflowers on a sunny windowsill. Plants suitable for dyeing which may already be growing are goldenrod, barberry (piperidge), tansy, broom, raspberry, blackberry, hazelnut, fern, rhubarb, marsh marigold, and others. Privet hedge cuttings can also be used for yellow and olive-green wool.

Nettles (a source of food for butterflies) can also be used for dyeing yellow-green wool. In late winter you can take a little bark from apple trees. Pine-cones — even last year's — can be used for dyeing.

Sorrel, plantain, milfoil and other herbs give nice colours. St-John's-wort can be found in summer. If it is not possible to gather enough of one plant to make a dye-bath you can mix different species. For instance, spinach and nettles, sorrel and plantain, goldenrod and birch leaves go well together. There is scope for experimentation.

When gathering leaves or plants for dyeing, pick them with care, leaving a good part of each plant so they are not damaged and can regenerate. *If you gather plants in the countryside make sure you are allowed to pick plants in the area, and that they are not endangered species.*

Some kinds of plants give a purer colour when they have been dried; others are better used when fresh. It is worth trying different possibilities. You will usually need double the amount of fresh plants compared to dried ones. It is normally not possible to tell whether a plant will give a good colour, what colour it will give, or which part of the plant to use, just by looking at it. Sometimes the colour can be found in the roots, e.g. rhubarb, madder; or in the bark and the

Figure 11. Marsh marigold dyes the wool orange-yellow.

Figure 12. Nettles give a yellow-green colour.

skins, e.g. onions and walnuts. Tagetes and marigolds are the exceptions because the flowers themselves are used.

After a while you might wish to use plants from outside your immediate environment. Plant dyes from other parts of the world can be purchased. The dyebaths described in this book are mainly from Northern and Central Europe. There are books which describe the whole dyeing process in more detail.

About the wool

More than any other fibre, sheep's wool absorbs plant dyes thoroughly and permanently. An old dyer once said: 'wool opens itself up, absorbs the plant pigments and holds them as tight as a jewellery setting holds a precious stone.'

A visit to the sheep farm

Try to make magic wool from beginning to end at least once, starting with a visit to a sheep farm. There may be several different kinds of sheep, and if you can, buy a bit of each wool type to get to know its quality and uses.

Long-stapled wool is good for winding dolls, short-stapled and curly more for pictures or carded mats where the wool is used in one piece.

Write down the type of wool used for each task for future reference. Try and arrange a visit during the shearing time. It is amazing how much wool comes off a single sheep! While the outside of the fleece is full of hay, bits of plant and dust and thus a grey-yellow, the inside is completely clean and ivory coloured. The fleece stays warm for a surprising length of time. It appears to be wet but this is the high amount of lanolin which glistens in a myriad of fine, golden drops.

Figure 13. Children with sheep.

Figure 14. Two freshly sheared sheep.

17

Sorting of the wool

Once at home lay out the wool and sort it. Separate about 200 g (7 oz) of the most beautiful parts of the fleece from the rest, and carefully tease all the dirt out. Unwashed and from healthy sheep, this 'therapeutic wool' has been used for a range of ailments for millennia — it can ease the pain of, for example, rheumatism, earache, sinusitis, simply by laying it on the skin.

Remove the dirt from the rest of the wool. Cut off yellowed and dirty tips. Tease the wool to fluff it up.

Figure 16. The wool is laid on the grass. On the left is the clean skin side of the wool.

Figure 15. Therapeutic wool.

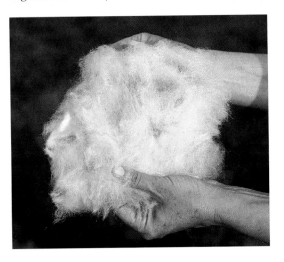

Washing the wool

Do not wash more than 1 kg (2 lb) at a time. About 100 g (3½ oz) of soap is needed depending how dirty the wool is. Grate the soap into a pot with a little hot water to dissolve it, and pour it into a tub with enough warm water (30°–40°C, 85°–105°F) so that the wool can float. Leave the fleece for about 30 minutes so that the dirt can loosen and then carefully wash it by squeezing it. Then rinse it three times in lukewarm water, Leaving it for about 20 minutes in each rinse.

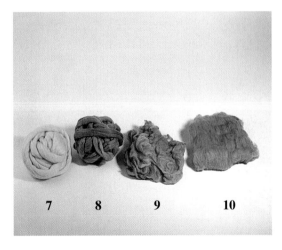

Figures 17–19.
  1. Unwashed raw wool
  2. Washed
  3. Dyed
  4. Teased
  5. Carded (drum carder)
  6. Carded (hand carders)
  7. Raw wool (roving from a shop)
  8. Dyed
  9. Teased
  10. Carded

Usually the wool is still too greasy to take the colour and a second cycle of washing is necessary. The wool will dry faster if you tie it into a pillowcase and spin it in a washing machine. After drying the wool in a shady place, it is ready for the mordant and dye.

If you can collect rainwater, soak the wool in it overnight before washing. Rainwater is also good for rinsing. If washing the wool in the bath use a sieve over the drain to prevent it blocking.

Mordanting

Wool needs to be prepared for dyeing by mordanting with alum or tartar as this makes the colours washable and light resistant. Always dissolve the mordant in cold water. You cannot reuse the mordant. Both in a mordant and a dye-bath there should be enough water so that the wool can float. Do not boil the wool, but let it simmer gently, stirring it carefully now and again.

Mordants

Alum is a white soluble salt. It intensifies and fixes all colours. Alum is the most versatile and most-used mordant.

Cream of tartar (Tatarus deporatus) fixes shades of red and violet as well as keeping the wool soft.

Tartaric acid (Cristalus tatari) has the consistency of white sugar and is used for shades of red.

Other helpful substances that can be used in conjunction with those mentioned above are:

Wheat germ: helps reds to appear purer.

Potash: makes colours towards gold and rust.

Cider vinegar: changes shades of red to violet.

Dyeing

Dyeing unspun wool is easier than dyeing spun wool or cloth which needs even colouring. Unspun, magic wool, on the other hand, becomes more alive through such irregularities in colour. Apart from that, carding can help even out the colour, and magic wool does not undergo much wear and tear. As nothing can really go wrong, have the courage to experiment!

The following recipes all refer to 500 g (1 lb) of wool. Prepare the dyes with fresh water.

Orange-yellow from marsh marigold

❖ *2 kg (4½ lb) of marsh marigold, whole plants*
   60 g (2 oz) alum, 30 g (1 oz) cream of tartar

Cut them up, soak them for 1–2 hours, simmer for an hour and strain off the marigolds to get a clear dye-bath.

Mordanting: Simmer for an hour, let the wool cool off in the mordant-bath.

Dyeing: Put the mordanted wool in the lukewarm dye-bath, bring slowly to the boil and simmer for an hour.

Figure 20. Dyer from Nuremberg c. 1500.

Figure 21-23. Plant-dyed, carded fleeces of wool.

Yellow with a hint of green from nettles

❖ 1–2 kg (2–4 lb) nettles
  60 g (2 oz) alum

Make the dye-bath in the same way as marsh marigold.

Mordanting: Proceed as for marsh marigold.

Dyeing: See dyeing marsh marigold.

Light green from nettles and indigo paste

Mordant and dye as described for yellow from nettles above. Take the wool out of the dye-bath. Add a few drops of indigo paste to the dye-bath and stir well.

Return the wool and simmer for a further 30 minutes.

The high quality blue dye *indigo* comes from an Indian type of fern. It is usually sold as an insoluble powder. Indigo paste is made out of a mixture of natural indigo powder and sulphuric acid and can be purchased. A few drops will change yellow into green. If you want to dye larger amounts of wool 'real' blue you will need to use the powder. Get a detailed book about dyeing for more information.

Golden-yellow from goldenrod

❖ *1.5 kg (3 lb) goldenrod*
  50 g (1¾ oz) alum
  20 g (¾ oz) cream of tartar
Use the whole plant shortly before it flowers, prepare the dye-bath as for marsh marigold.
  Mordanting: Simmer for an hour.
  Dyeing: Simmer for an hour.

Golden-yellow from onion skins

❖ *about 1 kg (2 lb) onion skins*
  50 g (1¾ oz) alum
  20 g (¾ oz) cream of tartar
Mordanting: Simmer for 1 hour.
  Dyeing: Put the wool and dried onion skins with a handful of copper coins into the dyeing pot, simmer for an hour, let the wool cool in the dye-bath overnight.

Light green from spinach

❖ *2 kg (4½ lb) finely-cut spinach*
  50 g (1¾ oz) alum
Ideally sow an extra amount of spinach early in spring. Harvest it before it shoots. The nice green colour comes from the high iron content. Boil the spinach for an hour and pour off the water the next day.

  Mordanting: Simmer for an hour.
  Dyeing: Simmer for an hour.

Beige with a tinge of red from green horse-chestnut husks

❖ *2 kg (4½ lb) of fresh chestnut husks*
Soak them for 1–2 days, preferably in rainwater, then boil them for 2 hours, let them cool and pour off the water.
  Mordanting is not necessary due to the natural mordant in the husks.
  Dyeing: Simmer for an hour. Put a handful of copper coins into the dye-bath.

Bright pink from cochineal lice

❖ *20 g (¾ oz) of ground cochineal*
  30 g (1 oz) tartaric acid
  20 g (¾ oz) alum
Real red, pink and violet shades are achieved by dyeing with cochineal lice. Originally from Mexico, this type of lice is bred on prickly pears. Only the females contain the precious dye.
  Mix the cochineal with some water and leave it overnight.
  Mordanting: Simmer for an hour.
  Dyeing: Stir the cochineal paste into cold water. Add the wool and simmer for an hour.

Light pink

❖ 15 g (½ oz) tartaric acid
10 g (just over ¼ oz) alum
Reuse the above dye-bath for 250 g (1 lb) wool.

Mordanting: Simmer for an hour.
Dyeing: Simmer for an hour.

Brick red from madder roots

❖ 250 g (½ lb) madder
200 g (7 oz) wheat germ
60 g (2 oz) alum
10 g (just over ¼ oz) tartaric acid
The root of madder is a classic dye from the Mediterranean. The roots can be purchased ready ground. Do not boil madder otherwise it will loose its red colour.

Mordanting: Simmer gently for an hour. Keep the wool in the remainder of the mordant for 3–4 days.

Dyeing: Tie the madder in a cloth bag and soak overnight. Leave the bag in the dye-bath throughout the dyeing process. Heat for an hour at c. 70°C (160°F), add the wheat germ.

The dye-bath will seldom be used up after one dyeing process. It can still be used for dyeing pink wool. Bring the dye-bath to the boil briefly to make a brown pink.

Rinsing

After dyeing, the cooled wool should be rinsed 3–5 times and dried in a shady spot.

Dyeing with natural dyes is not always predictable. The same recipe used at a different time of year or in different regions will give different shades. Climatic differences, water hardness, the greasiness of the wool, can all influence the finished colour. Some dyers claim that their mood also affects the colour. This just shows that dyeing is a living activity that can always produce surprises.

Teasing

Be careful with the washed and dyed wool. Do not rip or tear it apart, but carefully tease it. Take a small amount of wool between thumb and finger and gently pull apart the fibres. Teased wool is often nice enough to use directly as magic wool. Use any curly bits for gnomes' beards or dolls' hair.

Carding by hand

If the material needs to be more even (wound dolls, braided head-bands, gnomes etc.), card the wool after teasing. A hand carder consists of many fine wire hooks attached to a leather mat which is stapled to a wooden rectangle with a handle. They come in pairs.

Spread a small handful of wool lengthwise onto one of the carders. Hold the carder in your left hand, resting it on your left knee, and with the right hand stroke the empty carder gently over the first board. Take care not to pull diagonally or to let the hooks get caught in each other.

While carding, the fibres become even and smooth. When the right carder is full, turn it around so that both handles are facing the same way. Then push the right hand carder across the left — the wool will form a sausage or rolag. For a smoother result, spread the rolag onto the left carder and repeat the process.

Figure 24. Hand carders and drum carder.

Carding with a drum-carder

You can make big, evenly-carded fleeces with a drum-carder machine. Long strands of wool detached from it are very suitable for making figures. The machine has two drums, a smaller and a bigger one, joined by a belt. The rows of hooks point in opposite directions without touching.

Put a handful of well-teased wool onto the wooden board in front of the smaller drum. Turn the handle clockwise — the wool is pulled under the small drum and up between the two drums, where it is carded. While one hand turns the handle, the other feeds small, teased tufts of wool into the carder. Soon an evenly-carded fleece is deposited on the bigger drum.

To remove the fleece, lever a screwdriver under the wool at the seam of the bigger drum where there are no hooks. With a bit of gentle manoeuvering the fleece can be removed intact.

Instructions

Small birds

Make a small, very firm ball by winding white wool tightly into a ball. Lay a thick layer of wool around it and bind off the head (like the baby, see page 44). Fluff up the body, twisting the wool for the tail between forefinger and thumb. Pull out

Figure 25. Small birds.

the beak carefully with a needle. Insert two feathers for the wings.

If every child at the party or kindergarten group hangs their birds on a stick, they can all flock outside — maybe accompanied by a song — and greet the spring.

Figure 26. Flock of birds.

Figure 27. How to make light balls.
Figure 28. Mobile out of balls.

Light balls

Wind some colourful, long-stapled wool around a rectangular piece of card. Bind a thread through the top and bottom ends and sew in the thread. Pull the wool off the card and form it into a ball. These delicate balls, which are much stronger than they look, encourage all kinds of play.

To make a mobile, hang several balls from a stick or a ring as shown. If you hang a small bell in the centre of the ball, so that it remains invisible, the mobile will tinkle in the wind.

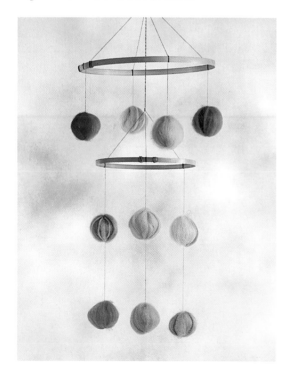

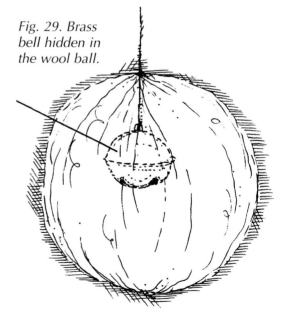

Fig. 29. Brass bell hidden in the wool ball.

Easter rabbit

❖ *15 g (½ oz) fleece of long-stapled*
   wool, c. 70 cm (28″) long

These simple rabbits are made out of two knots. Tighten the head knot a little more than the body knot. Separate the tip of the head knot and make into two ears. Tuck the other end into the body knot, to make the tail. You can add a little Easter egg on the back.

Do not leave the ears too long, or it will look unnatural.

Smaller rabbits can be made in the same way from shorter fleeces; the tail end can be pushed into the body knot with a needle.

Figures 31 and 32. Easter rabbits made out of two knots.

Figure 30.

1. *Tie headknot tightly, dividing tuft into two ears.*

2. *Loosely tie body-knot below head.*

3. *Tuck end into body to make tail.*

29

Figure 33. Flowers.

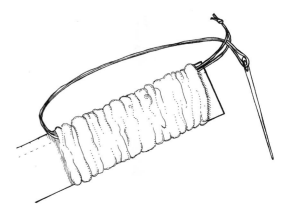

Figure 34. Making the flower rosette.

Flowers

Evenly wind a thin layer of very long-stapled wool for about 20 cm (8″) around a ruler that is not more than 3 cm (1¼″) wide. Thread a needle and knot the ends of the thread together. Push the needle through the inside of the wool tube, bunch up the wool and push it off the ruler. Insert the needle into the loop of thread at the end, pull the tube together, sew in the ends and the simple flower rosette is finished (see Figures 33 and 36).

Flower centre and stalk

Wind some yellow wool around one end of a pipe-cleaner. Loop that end over to make the centre of the flower. Stick the pipe-cleaner through the middle of the flower rosette, so the yellow loop is the centre of the flower and the end of the pipe-cleaner is the stalk. Then wrap green wool tightly around the stalk.

Variation

A fuller flower can be made when a smaller rosette is placed on top of a larger one. Make them using a thinner and thicker ruler.

The fine stripes in Figure 33 come from very thin pieces of long-stapled wool.

Figure 35. Lisa with a braided head band and flower.

Figure 36. Simple flowers.

To make tiny flowers wind the wool around smaller strips of card.

Woollen flowers have many uses. Lots of big flowers with stalks make a nice bunch. Single flowers can adorn a headband. Small flowers without a stalk transform a green wool meadow into a flowery carpet or can be attached to the clothes of the dolls. Children can make colourful armbands by sewing lots of small flowers onto a wide elastic.

Pom-pom rabbits

❖ *30 g (1 oz) of wool*

Wind the wool strands around both of the oval card pieces to make a pom-pom (see Figure 40 and 42). After wrapping wool round both oval stencils, cut along the edge and tie a strong thread tightly around the centre between the card-board stencils. Pull off the cardboard. Cut the pom-pom along the bottom to make it flat. Shape the head by cutting a neck with a small, very sharp pair of scissors. The clever bit of these rabbits are the felt ears with their pink lining.

Lay two thin layers of wool — one the colour of the fur, and the other pink — on top of each other. Rub them between

Figure 37. Pom-pom rabbits.

both palms with soap and warm water. After a few minutes the wool will have loosely felted. Cut the ears out of this and sew them on while the felt is still wet, shaping them into a typical ear form. One of the rabbits is made of brown-black alpaca wool, the other one of sheep's wool dyed with onion skin.

A pom-pom hedgehog

❖ *30 g (1 oz) of very greasy wool, 2 pipe-cleaners (1 for the head and front legs, 1 for the tail and back legs)*

Make the pom-pom in the same way as the rabbits. Wind strands of wool along the whole length of both pipe-cleaners. Bend them as shown in Figure 38. Wind more wool around the bent forms to

shape them. Sew the pieces tightly onto the flattened bottom of the pom-pom. Twist lots of spines out of the pom-pom with your fingertips; this only works with greasy wool, otherwise use some lanolin to grease the wool. Embroider on a pink nose.

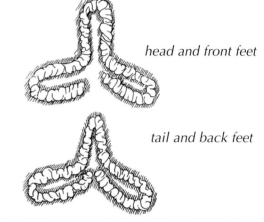

head and front feet

tail and back feet

Figure 38. Hedgehog's head, feet and tail

Figure 39. Pom-pom hedgehog.

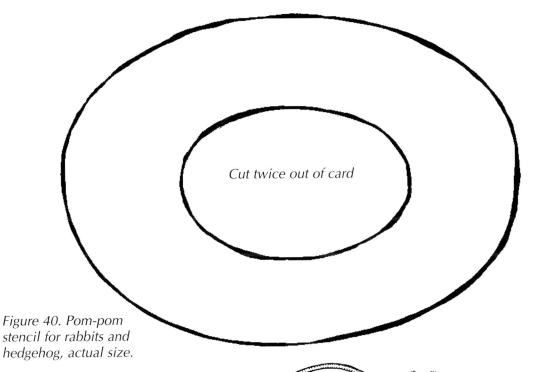

Cut twice out of card

Figure 40. Pom-pom stencil for rabbits and hedgehog, actual size.

Figure 41. This shows how the head, legs and tail have been attached.

Figure 42. Pom-pom partially cut open.

33

Basic body

The instructions below are for different standing dolls, for example the Season's Fairies (see page 73), for playing and dolls house dolls, as well as for a season's table.

❖ *c. 20 g (¾ oz) of very long-stapled wool in skin colour.*
Height of the doll is about 16 cm (6")

1. Make a very firm ball out of skin-coloured wool with a circumference of about 10 cm (4"). Lay two layers of skin-coloured wool in a cross on top of each other.

Put the ball in the middle, fold all the strands together, and bind off the head tightly and smoothly using a double thread. Wind around the neck repeatedly. Always sew the threads in well. Leave a threaded needle (with a knot at the end) near at hand so that you do not have to lay down the work at any time.

2. Separate the strands of wool for the arms from the body. Decide on the length of the arms (otherwise the doll cannot hold the baby) and double back the arm strands. For the hand lay a small, tight ball in the fold of the arm and bind off.

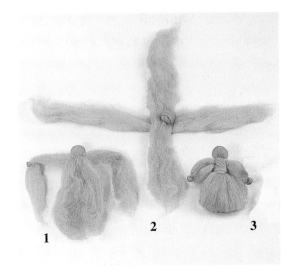

Figure 43. Making the basic body.

3. Fold up the body strand to the length of the skirt and bind everything — the ends of the arm wool and the top of the skirt — tightly around the waist. The basic figure is finished.

To dress the doll, start with the arms. Wind a long, thin strand of wool firmly round the arm from wrist to shoulder. It doesn't matter if the wool gets twisted. Wind the wool right up to the last fibres to save you sewing it in. Wind a second, thin strand of wool around the arm from top to bottom, without twisting, winding the last fibres into the wrist.

Check that both arms are the same length, and that they get thinner towards the wrists.

Dress the back and chest next. Tease out the end of the coloured strand of wool you are going to use to make it thinner and wind it around the neck a few times, then firmly wind it crosswise over the chest and back, and lastly wind it round the waist. There should be no more 'skin' showing.

Giant snails

❖ *15–20 g (½ –¾ oz) long-stapled wool, thin card*

Loosely wind a length of wool c. 65 cm (25") long into the form of a spiral snail shell and sew together at the bottom with a few stitches. Leave the needle and thread attached.

Make the body from a card rectangle, 17 x 5 cm (6½" x 2"), rounding off the corners. Wind wool around the card first lengthwise then widthwise. Sew on the shell with a few stitches and remove the needle. To make the stalks thread a length of thick yarn through the head, then knot both ends. Bend the head end up slightly.

These giant snails are easily made and can be used not only for decoration (for example on a birthday table, or as a present), but also to play the following game.

Snail race

Each player gets a 'racing snail' that is attached to a long string (all the same length). Attach wooden handles at the end of these strings for winding them up. Before the beginning of the race tuck a nut or cookie under the snails' house. The players all start winding their snails

Figure 44. Snails.

towards themselves at the same time. If anybody's snail falls over they have to start again. There are no losers in this game, as in the end everyone gets to have their little reward.

Butterflies

Light, airy magic wool lends itself to making colourful butterflies, though the bulkiness of the wool does not really suit a butterfly. Nevertheless, to make thin, translucent wings place two very thin differently coloured layers of wool, about palm-size, on top of each other. Gently rub them between both palms with warm water and soap. After a few minutes, sometimes only seconds, a fine,

Figure 45. Snail race (water colour).

transparent felt is made. When held against the light fine veins can be seen in the wings, like a real butterfly.

Cut both wings out of this. Cut the butterfly wider than seems necessary, as you loose nearly 1 cm (½″) when the body is sewn in. With a few stitches sew a thick piece of yarn into the centre fold for the body. Divide the yarn at the top and twist the feelers between thumb and index finger.

Figure 47. Butterflies on a thistle.

Figure 46. Pattern for the butterfly (50% of actual size)

Figure 48. Yarn sewn in the centre fold for the body.

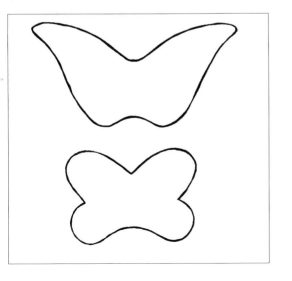

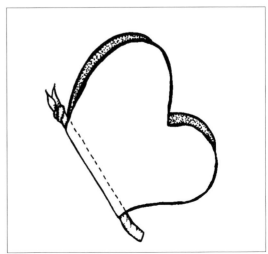

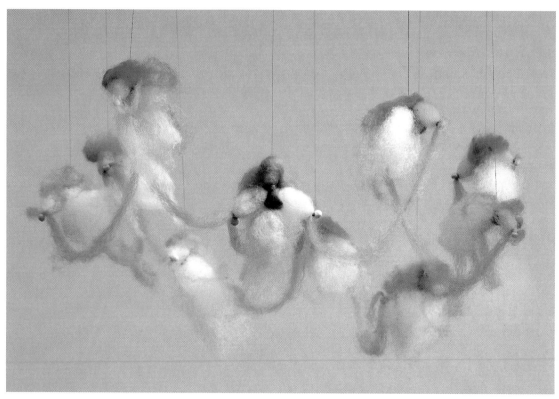

Figures 49–51. Sylph mobile; the sylphs move with any breath of wind.

Sylphs

❖ *15 g (½ oz) of wool*
See the Birds (page 27) and the Basic Body (page 34) for instructions how to bind off head and hands.

With blue wool wind crosswise sparingly over chest and back. Sew on blue hair. Tease the hair and dress to make it look windblown.

Sylph mobile

For a 'sylph dance' hang up a few figures on a ring (wood, wire or willow twigs bent to make a circle). Each fairy is looking outwards and has enough room around itself to move freely (Figure 49). Finish by connecting the hanging figures with soft blue long-stapled wool strands attached to the wrists.

Hang the sylph mobile from the ceiling, not too low. The ring onto which they are fastened should be able to rotate. The best place for the mobile is either the children's room or the living room. If there is a window nearby the slightest draft will make the fairies dance.

Rainbow fairy

The rainbow fairy is made similarly to the sylphs. The upper body is not wound, apart from the waist. Pull thin, long-stapled wool in all colours of the rainbow through the waist-band (see Basic Body, page 34, and Pipe-cleaner Dolls, page 40). Lay colourful strands of wool onto a layer of white wool, wind it around the head and sew it on, to make the hair. Form and tease the figure so that it appears to be floating.

Figure 52. Rainbow fairy.

Pipe-cleaner dolls

These pipe-cleaner dolls are suitable both for a dolls house or a seasonal table.

❖ *3 pipe-cleaners*
  20–30 g (¾–1 oz) of long-stapled wool
1. First wind a small, very tight ball for the head, (see also Basic Body, page 34 and Birds page 27). Lay skin-coloured wool smoothly over it, bind off the head with thread and sew the ends in well.

2. Divide the body wool into four strands for each arm and leg.

3. Bend the pipe-cleaners into arms and legs as shown, and wind the strands of wool around them densely and tightly. Ensure that the arms and legs get thinner towards the wrists and ankles. Bend the ends of the arms and legs into loops for the hands and feet. These loops should be filled with the ends of the strands of wool (use a big needle).

Dolls can be wound entirely out of skin colour. Their clothes can either be made out of removable cloth, or make the last layer of wool a different colour, as in the example below.

Figure 53. The stages of process.

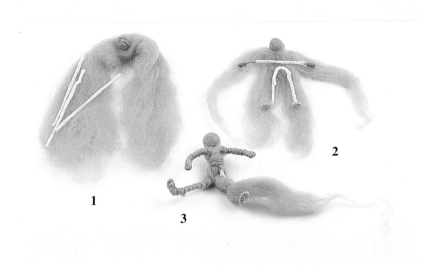

4. Wind the wool crosswise around the chest and back. For the trousers place a thin tuft of wool between the legs like a diaper or nappy and wind around the top to secure it.

5. The basic hairstyle is made by sewing a little bit of wool onto the head with small stitches. To make the doll more durable, felt the surface. Dip the whole figure into hot water. With thoroughly soaped hands massage the doll for about 20 minutes, as if trying to wash it well. Then rinse it out properly, spin it in the washing machine, and let it dry in a warm place.

6. To finish, some loose wool is sewn on top of the felted hair to create the desired hairstyle. Mouth and eyes can be embroidered on. The skirt of the girl below is made out of strands of wool that were pulled through the waist. Make sandals to allow the figures to stand. Cut the sole out of card (not to small), and fasten it to the foot with yarn as sandal straps.

Figure 54. The stages of process.

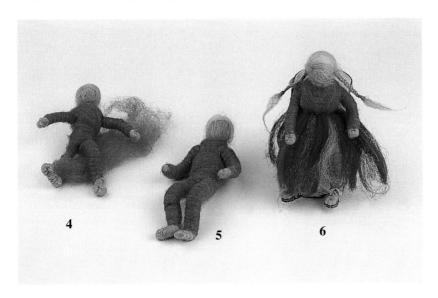

41

Doll mother with baby

The dolls with swaddled babies are particularly popular with young mothers, as they bring good luck.

Make the body as described under Basic Body on page 34.

1. For the skirt, wind a wide, thick layer of wool around the doll, not too loosely! The dress should get slightly wider towards the base, if necessary wind another thin layer around it.

2. To make the folds or stripy pattern, take a few long, thin strands of wool that complement the colour of the dress. With the help of a thick needle pull the strands through the waist of the doll and distribute them evenly around the skirt.

3. Now hold the doll upside down between your knees. Gather all the strands together, twist them into one big strand and thread it into a big, long needle. Stick the needle into the centre of the base of the doll and pull this strand inside. The doll will stand securely if a twisted cord or a braid is sewn around the hem of the skirt (Figure 56).

Figure 55. The stages of making a doll mother.

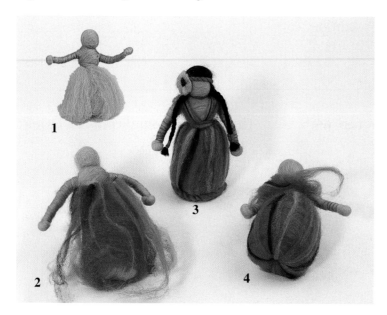

Figure 56. The base of the doll showing how to finish off.

Figure 57. Doll mothers with swaddled babies.

4. The blouse can be trimmed with thin stripes down the sleeves, a shawl and a belt. Do the hair last. Put the doll between your knees again so that both hands are free. Lay the wool firmly and smoothly around the head and sew it on with lots of tiny stitches. Depending on the desired style either sew a parting or sew from ear to ear. Tease some wool over any visible stitches.

These dolls are sturdier than they may seem, as long as they have been made carefully. Over time the surface becomes felted through repeated touching, which makes them even more durable. If you want an especially long-lasting doll, strengthen critical spots (arms, shoulders, waist, base) with small stitches.

Figure 58. Dolls with rabbit and small sheep.

Figure 59. Swaddled baby.

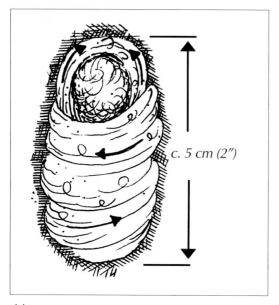

c. 5 cm (2")

Swaddled baby

Wind a small, pink firm ball for the head of the baby. Lay a thick layer of wool firmly over it and tie off the neck. If the body is too long, bend it up and wind the ends around the neck. Wind the swaddling clothes first lengthways around the head and feet, and then across the body like a blanket. Wind the strand to the very end and tuck in.

If the arms of the mother doll have been wound firmly and long enough, they can be bent to hold the baby securely.

Miniature roses

Tease a small strand of green wool and knot it in the middle. Roll a small red tuft into a ball between thumb and index finger for the blossom. Wet the tuft slightly, to felt and hold better. Stick a needle with thread through both the green knot and the ball and bring the needle back out again just beside it to make a tiny stitch.

Figure 60. A family of bendy dolls at a table.

Gnomes

Gnomes are little elemental creatures, usually invisible to us. So, to invite these mysterious characters into our hosue, we need some patience. Together with the children we can choose a place and think of what a gnome might need — roots, bits if bark, stones, dry leaves, cloths, wool, and so on. We might make a simple table out of birch bark, a bed out of moss and provide a basket with nuts and berries. Maybe even a tiny jug for water can be found somewhere in the house (see, for example, Figure 61).

A 'real' gnome will not just come overnight, so at first the children will have to wait patiently. Only when he is happy with his home and is sure to be welcomed will he appear some day. While waiting, children like hearing stories and verses about gnomes. One morning the gnome will be found in his corner, shy and somewhat hidden. Children are quick to feel that there is something 'mysterious' about this character and so will not treat it the same as other toys (like dolls or soft animals).

The gnome's world comes to life

Adults need to ensure that the gnome's corner keeps changing and does not become messy — they must make sure that the gnome actually 'eats' the nuts that are left for him. Treasures that are found during a walk, for example a beautiful feather, a snail's shell or the shimmering wing of a beetle can be brought back as a present for the gnome.

In the morning it is sometimes possible to see how the gnome has been busy in the night, rearranging his area. On other occasions he just sleeps for days on end in his moss bed.

At least once a year he gets ready for his journey into the depths of the earth, to take part in the big gathering of gnomes. The children can tell when this time comes by his bundle, which lies ready at the entrance of his corner a few days in advance. Then the gnome disappears for a few weeks. When he eventu-

Figure 61. A cheeky gnome, sitting comfortably in a basket of magic wool.

ally comes back he might bring back a tiny letter from the king of the gnomes, or a precious stone or even maybe a companion. Often he comes back on a particular day, for example the birthday of one of the members of the family, or at a point when one of the children need special attention.

When making the gnome's area 'to his liking,' try to find natural materials like bark, roots, leaves (in the picture there are dried rose leaves), moss, pine brushwood, and so on. Some of the pictured pine-cones have been coloured with gold-bronze paint.

The story of the moss-woman

Many years ago, in the Bavarian woods near Passau, there still lived the moss-folk. They were like tiny gnomes, and they wore clothes and skirts out of moss and aprons out of pine brushwood. They lived in holes in the ground under moss-grown stones or in hollow tree-trunks. Their biggest enemy was the Wild Hunter; whenever he saw one of them while out hunting he would chase them.

One day a young woodcutter espied one of the moss-women. She was sitting on a tree stump and throwing beechnuts at a squirrel, which was peeking out from behind the trunk of a spruce-tree. Every time one of the nuts came flying, the animal ducked behind the tree. The moss-woman thought that was so funny she laughed out loud each time it happened.

The woodcutter watched this scene for a short while, and then decided to catch the moss-woman; silently he crept up to her, but just as he reached out to catch her she jumped away.

So the young man went back to work, swung his axe and sawed all day until evening. Then he wanted to go home.

Suddenly he saw the moss-woman standing a few steps in front of him again, and she lifted her hands and implored him: 'Don't go home before you have cut three crosses into every felled tree, otherwise we are lost.'

'Why should you be lost?' the wood-cutter asked.

The moss-woman answered: 'Don't you know that the Wild Hunter is after us? Whenever he catches one of us he kills her. Only when we're sitting on a tree stump that has three crosses notched into it are we safe.'

The woodcutter felt sorry for the tiny creature, and cut three clear crosses into every tree he had felled. When he had finished doing so, moss-women and moss-men came out from the darkness of the wood towards him from all sides, and every one of them gave him a shining pine-cone. 'Take these in payment for saving us from the Wild Hunter!' they called. 'We will never forget what you have done for us.'

Although there were plenty of pine-cones lying on the forest ground, the woodcutter didn't want to hurt their feelings, and so he thanked them for the presents and put them in his bag. Then he went home.

At home he wanted to put the pine-cones straight into the shed. To his

Figure 62. Moss-woman and moss-man in the forest. Their hats are held under their arms.

Figure 63. The realm of the moss-folk with a pet hedgehog (see page 32).

surprise it was not dry brown pine-cones that fell out of his bag, but lots of golden ones. The woodcutter sold them and received so much money, that he could live happily ever after.

Instructions for Making Gnomes

Moss-folk

❖ c. *50 g (1¾ oz) wool, (20 g, ¾ oz of
   that in skin colour for the basic
   form),*
   4 pipe-cleaners
The figure is *c.* 15 cm (6") high without
his hat.

Making gnomes requires some experience of working with magic wool. Leave
enough time for the production and
arrangement of these figures. To main-
tain the mystery of gnomes, children
should not watch while they are being
made, especially as during production
the figures can look unnatural and vul-
nerable. If children are to be included,
they can choose the wool for the clothes
and lay it out. Later, when the boots and
hat are being felted, they can join in
again.

Figure 64. The inside of a moss-folk figure.

Heads and legs

Make a very firm ball out of skin-
coloured wool with a circumference of
about 12 cm (5"). The inside can be an
old ball of yarn. Then lay two thick layers of skin-coloured wool crosswise on
top of each other, tighten it smoothly
around the ball, and tie the neck off with
a strong thread (see Basic Body, page
34). Wrap the thread repeatedly around
the neck and sew the ends in well.

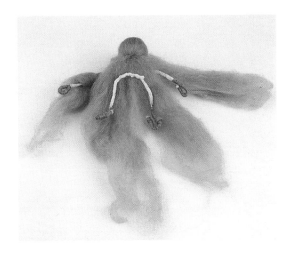

Figure 65. Moss-woman and moss-man.

Separate the bottom strand into four equal parts (for arms and legs). For the arms, twist two pipe-cleaners together, so that they have a combined length of *c.* 27 cm (11″), and bend the ends into loops for the hands (see also instructions for Pipe-cleaner Dolls, page 40).

Before bending the arms and feet bind some wool around that part of the pipe-cleaner. Wind the arm strands of wool firmly and densely around the arm pipe-cleaners. Ensure the arms are the same length. Fill the hand loops with the help of a long needle.

Make the legs in the same way. Make the loops for the feet quite a bit bigger than the loops for the hands.

The proportions of the gnome can already be seen: big head, long arms, short legs with big feet. In comparison to a pipe-cleaner doll (page 40) the difference is obvious.

The gnome still needs a slight hunchback. Take a tuft of wool and stuff it behind the back, horizontal pipe-cleaner. The stomach also needs an extra tuft of wool wound around it. Wind firmly and densely, crosswise around the whole body of the figure. It is better to wind lots of thin layers than a few thick ones.

Then wind around the upper body in the colour of the gnome's sweater; first the arms, getting thicker towards the shoulders, then the chest, back and waist. For the trousers wind around the legs, being careful not to make them too fat, and then around the lower body. To make dungarees: lay the wool between the legs like a diaper (nappy), separate the ends of the wool at the chest and the back and pull them over the shoulders like straps. With a new strand wind around the body like a belt to hold everything in place. Pull all the ends of the wool strands into the centre of the gnome with a needle.

The skirt

The moss-woman wears a skirt over her dungarees. To make it, wind some wool around a rectangular piece of card, 11 x 8 cm (4″ x 3″), (Figure 66), and felt it as

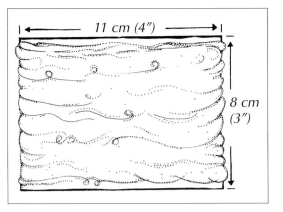

Figure 66. Pattern for felted skirt.

described on page 54 (hat and boots). Push the seamless basic form of the skirt off the card. Cut the bottom of the skirt in the shape of leaves or a fringe. Put the skirt on the figure and gather it just under the arms with thick thread.

Figure 67. Felted seamless skirt.

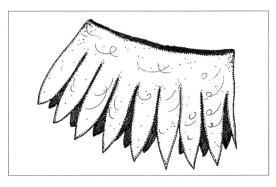

Basic check

Now is the time to look at the product with a critical eye: even if it does not look quite like imagined there is no reason to despair: at this stage much can be changed and improved.

Is the gnome chubby enough? If not, wind some more layers around it.

Are the proportions right; are the legs the same length; the arms?

The arms need to be longer than the legs. If necessary unwind some areas and correct them.

Although the figure should have a slight hunchback, it should not be curved to the side. If necessary adjust.

Are the feet carefully made and bent into a natural form? As the boots are removable the feet should be well-finished, otherwise do them again!

When everything is right, secure the whole figure with little stitches, to prevent anything slipping.

Nose and eyes

The big, round nose of the moss-folk is felted. Make a very tight little ball out of skin-coloured wool. With hot water and soap roll it between your palms for about 15 minutes. Sometimes it takes repeated attempts to achieve a round ball. Cut the ball in half with a sharp knife, (two noses are made at the same time).

Sew the nose with its flat side to the face of the gnome. Do not sew it too high up, as the gnome needs a high forehead.

Sew the mouth in dark red as a single line directly under the nose.

Sew the eyes as two squint lines right above the nose. Sew a bright blue small vertical line in the centre of the eye with embroidery thread. This gives the glint in the eye.

The hair and beard is made out of a single piece of wool: make a hole in the centre for the face and sew it onto the head with tiny stitches. Tease the wool to

make the hair fuller. Twist out lots of spikes from the hair and beard between forefinger and thumb. This will only work if the wool still contains enough grease, otherwise rub some lanolin into the hair between your fingertips.

Felted hat and boots

Now only the hat and boots are still missing. Again they are felted. Wind some magic wool broadly around the card pattern (see Figure 68 and 69), making sure there are no holes. Briefly dip the wound wool into hot water, and then soap it well. Rub the whole form between your hands, at first very carefully so that nothing slips. Always massage the soapy wool against the card edge, so that the form turns out well. It takes about 15 to 20 minutes per item.

Cut the hat open along the base (Figure 68) and take out the wet card. Rinse well. Decorate the hat with a pine twig.

A pair of boots are felted in one piece. Cut open along the dotted line (Figure 69) at the top of the legs. Remove the card and rinse out well. Put the boots on while they are still damp and mould them so that the gnome can stand in them. If necessary add card soles. If the legs are not quite the same size a layer of wool can be placed in one of the boots.

Figure 68. Pattern for the felt hat (actual size).

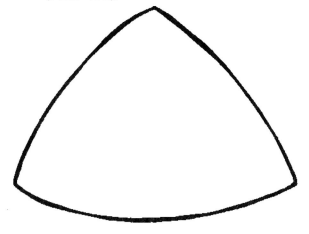

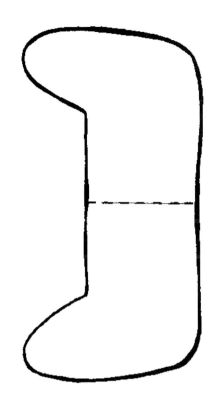

Plants used for gnomes pictured

Sweater, beard and hair: nettles, as well as nettles dyed again with a little bit of indigo.

Green boots and hat: birch leaves with a little bit of indigo.

Dungarees and skirts: onion skins redyed with logwood

Dark purple boots and hats: logwood.

Skin colour: onion skins redyed with a little bit of bark of black alder.

Figure 69. Pattern for the boots (actual size).

Two gnomes hiding

Hand-felted mat

❖ *70 g (2½ oz) of wool*
  card 45 x 34 cm (18″ x 13½″)

The finished picture will be a little smaller due to shrinkage from the felting.

These little gnomes live in a mountain landscape. Carded or well-teased wool in different green tones is used. Keep a handful aside. Lay the wool onto the card. Then put a small, separate triangle of card onto the part where the gnome cave will be (see pattern, Figure 70). Spread the remaining wool over it, making sure the card is not visible. This will prevent the wool of the hollow from being felted together. To ensure the 'entrance' does not felt shut slip your hand into the pocket every now and again while felting. When the whole piece is well felted, remove the small card piece and felt the inside of the pocket.

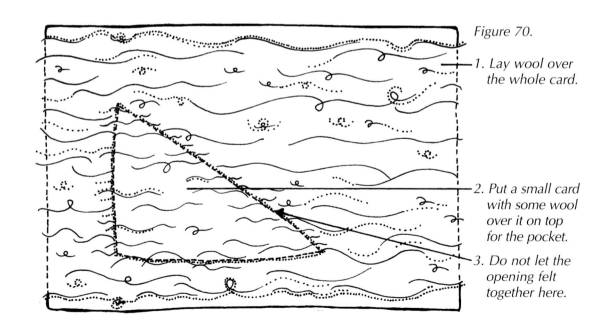

Figure 70.

1. Lay wool over the whole card.

2. Put a small card with some wool over it on top for the pocket.

3. Do not let the opening felt together here.

Figure 71. The finished mat. Note the opening of the hiding place. The trees are made of twigs with some wool wrapped around them and fastened to the felt with a few stitches.

Miniature gnomes

Each gnome only weighs about 5–10 g (¼ oz) and is about 7 cm (3") big with a pointed hat, and is made like a simple wound figure, without wire inside. Wind the figures using many very thin strands rather then a few thick ones.

1. Wind a small ball for the head.

2. Put a layer of skin-coloured wool over it.

3. Bind around the neck repeatedly with thread and sew in the ends.

4. Divide the wool into four parts and wind the arms and legs firmly.

Figure 72. The two miniature gnomes.

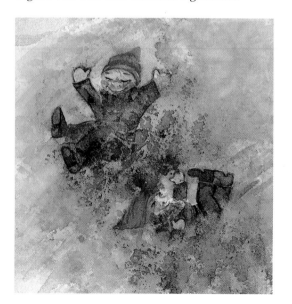

5. For the felted hat see 'red-capped gnomes', but make a smaller version.

To hang the picture, stretch a piece of silk over a cork-board which makes a nice background. Pin on the felted picture.

The landscape can easily be changed and enhanced by laying on more magic wool. Children enjoy doing this. The gnomes can hide behind a bush or tree, for example. In winter the green wool can be replaced by white wool creating a snowy landscape overnight with red hats peeping out.

Peter William Butterblow

Under the bright summer sun
what could be more fun
than to go searching far and wide
all along the warm hillside?

How soon the summer day will pass
with hunting through the hazy grass.
Take your jug or pot or cup:
don't stop until you fill it up.
And why do we spend these happy hours
searching amongst the meadow flowers?
To find wild strawberries ripe and red
for a supper snack with milk and bread.

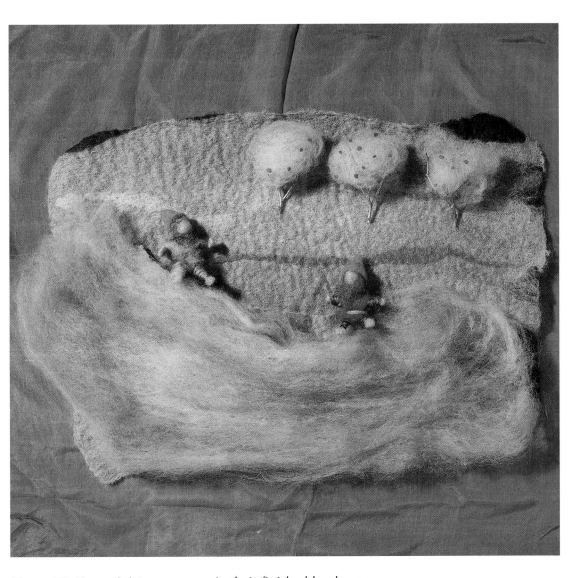

Figure 73. Two miniature gnomes in their finished landscape.

Figure 74. A landscape of snow can appear overnight by putting a layer of white wool over the picture.

Suggestion for games

During the day the gnome scene can hang on the wall like a normal magic wool picture, for instance above the child's bed. In the evening the merry gnomes can emerge to play all kinds of games. Remove the picture from the wall and lay it onto the bed. The gnomes' games can be accompanied with simple rhymes. At the end both the gnomes disappear back into their mountain, tired from all their playing, to go to bed. A reason, perhaps, for the children to do the same.

Red-capped or flower gnomes

Unlike the moss-gnomes which are primarily made with earthy forest colours, the red-capped or flower gnomes like bright colours. This can be seen by their colourful clothes and by the decoration of their surroundings: coloured flowers, fruits, silk cloths and precious stones. The red-capped gnomes are more delicate and less gnome-like and gnarled than the moss-gnomes, which make them appear younger.

❖ *30 – 40 g (1–1½ oz) wool, two pipe-cleaners*

The basic figure is described on page 34, Basic Body, and the legs are made like the Moss-folk, page 51. The head should be wound slightly bigger than the doll's, the arms, without wire, slightly longer. Wind a tuft of wool onto the back to make a hunchback. For the legs and feet twist two pipe-cleaners together to make a length of about 26 cm (10"). Wind the separated strands of leg-wool around the joined pipe-cleaners, bend big loops at the end for feet, then do everything else the same as the Moss-folk.

For the smock make a hole in a small layer of wool and pull it over the head of the gnome. A strand of long-stapled wool makes a belt. Hair and beard are likewise made out of a single layer of wool, tease a hole for the face and sew it onto the head.

In Figure 76 one of the gnomes is wearing felted boots and pointed hat. The boots are made as described for the Moss-folk.

Figure 75 is the pattern of the pointed hat. Bind some bright red wool around the card pattern, which should be slightly larger than the finished size of the hat. Dip the wound wool into hot water and felt it with soapy hands for about 15 minutes.

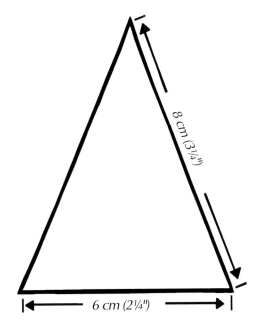

8 cm (3¼")

6 cm (2¼")

Figure 75. Pattern for the pointed hat for the red-capped gnomes.

Figure 76. Red-capped or flower gnomes.

Cut the hat opening, remove the card, rinse the hat well and sew it to the head.

The hat and boots of the second gnome are only wound and shaped by hand. Twist the end of the hat between forefinger and thumb. Wrap the boots around the feet and fasten them with lots of small stitches. Lastly, secure both figures with lots of small stitches, as with the moss-men.

Magic Wool and the Seasons

Three different possibilities to create a seasonal corner are described in this chapter.

If you do not have much space and would like to do felting, then make the *Seasonal Tree,* a picture that can hang on the wall. The tree's foliage can be changed from season to season.

You need more space to make a *Landscape* using bigger, coloured matted wool. With a few skilful twists of the hand, and a few little odds and ends a magical landscape for dolls and puppets can be created. Below, a seasonal tableau is described which can be set where the whole family will see it, for example in the living or dining room.

Making a *Season's Fairy* requires some experience in using magic wool. The figure itself, adorned suitably for the season, is happy with a small space on a shelf or table. Drape a shallow basket or bowl with a silk cloth, letting it fall over the edge. The colour of the cloth can change with the season. Place the figure

inside the bowl. On Sundays or special days the fairy can be on the dining room table. Beautiful backgrounds for the fairies are the landscapes mentioned above and described on pages 66–72.

Seasonal tree

The tree, as the main motif, is firmly felted into the hand-felted picture plane. Leaves, blossoms, fruit and everything around it are created season by season with magic wool, so that the tree can follow the seasons through the year.

Making the basic picture

❖ *40–50 g (1½ –1¾ oz) carded wool in blue and off-white, and some strands of long-stapled wool in different shades of brown, for a picture of about 30 x 26 cm (12" x 10")*

First cut out a rectangular piece of card about 2–3 cm (1") bigger all round than the desired picture. With a few pencil lines draw the basic form of the tree, the

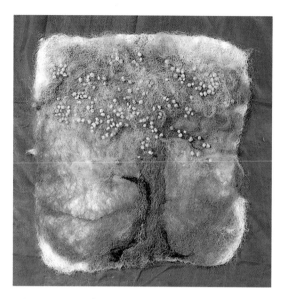

Figures 77. The season's tree in full flower in spring.

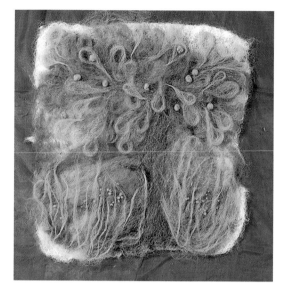

Figure 78. Summer: the tree is in abundant green.

trunk, branches and twigs, but no leaves as these will be added loosely afterwards.

'Paint' the tree with wool in different shades of brown: wet every strand of wool and brush it onto the card like a paint stroke. It will stay in position because it is wet. Take time for this process, and change the picture until it is exactly right.

Then lay carded blue-white wool in one piece on top, right across the tree (we begin by working the back of the picture). This mat should be evenly carded or teased without any holes.

Felting: Pour some hot water (*c.* 40°C, 105°F) into the centre and scatter soap flakes or shavings on top. Then carefully rub the surface with a flat hand, starting at the centre. Press the wool onto the base, so that the soapy water gets distributed evenly. If necessary add water and soap. The soapsuds should have the consistency of whipped cream.

Ensure that the wool doesn't get rubbed off the card. Push it back now and again, and rub from the outside to the centre more often than vice versa. Watch that the piece is worked through evenly

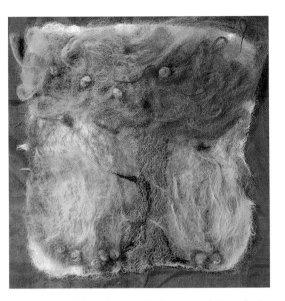

Figure 79. Windswept foliage and ripe fruit in autumn.

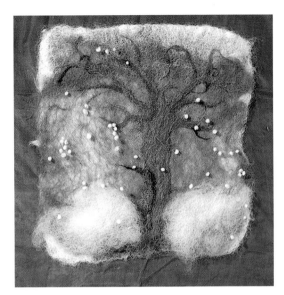

Figure 80. Winter: the felted form of the tree is visible.

in all directions. The raw felt will always shrink in the direction it is rubbed.

If necessary squeeze out water that has cooled and substitute with warm water. Add more soap if your hand no longer glides smoothly over the wool. Although the whole thing should be wet through, it should never be swimming in water. It is possible to feel the wool becoming firmer and more stable through the process of felting.

After about 20 minutes peel the mat off the card and turn it around. Usually the form of the tree is so stable that it is now possible to work from the front without the picture slipping. If in doubt turn it over again and felt some more. Lastly rinse it out well, smooth it and let it dry on a towel.

Changing the tree through the year

Spring
Tease and form light green leaves out of wool and strew lots of small pink wool balls as blossoms over them. Lastly lay a very fine layer of white or pink wool over the foliage.

Summer

Drape thick leaves in different shades of green around the branches, a rainbow is hinted at in the sky, high grass is growing around the tree.

Autumn

The foliage is colourful now. Fruit hangs from the branches; some has fallen and is lying on the ground. The leaves are swept by the autumn wind.

Winter

The tree is bare. The basic felted form is visible. Frost is lying on the branches, snowflakes are falling.

Let the added magic wool (leaves, rainbow etc.) protrude beyond the felted base. The whole picture becomes less enclosed.

To mount the picture see Two Gnomes Hiding (page 56).

Landscapes

Even when the children are older there can still be a place for an atmospheric seasonal corner. The pictures here are simply examples to stimulate your own creativity. The important thing is to represent the typical aspects of the seasons as simply as possible. Whole carded fleeces make the landscape look more extensive.

The fleeces in the pictures have been carded very evenly with a drum-carder. The weight is about 50 g (1¾ oz). Alternatively fairly even fleeces can be made through patient teasing.

Springtime

There is a shepherd with flock, a bower in bloom behind, and the meadow is made of different shades of green wool hanks.

See instructions for Basic Body, page 34, to make the shepherd.

Knitted sheep

❖ *15 g (½ oz) off-white wool yarn*
  teased unspun wool
  2 knitting needles
Knit (garter stitch) the body of the sheep, following the pattern below.

Fold the edge marked O and sew

Figure 81. Spring landscape.

bind off edge together on wrong side of the work.

With a few gathering stitches, bring **X** to meet **A** at each side, pulling slightly as you stitch. Shape the resulting ears with a few stitches.

Sew wrong sides of the leg seams and body seams, leaving the rear open for stuffing.

Turn to right side, stuff the sheep firmly with teased wool beginning with the legs: use one hand to shape the body while the other hand stuffs it. Sew up the stuffing hole at the back.

Sew on a crocheted cord for a tail.

Bower

Soak thin willow twigs and form them into a bower. Wind green magic wool around them loosely. The twigs are pressed into a horse-shoe shaped roll of not quite dry clay. Do not roll the clay too thin, otherwise it will not be able to stand the pressure of the twigs. Twist white blossoms out of bits of fluff and lay them onto a very fine green wool veil, where they will stick. Wind this blossom veil around the front twig.

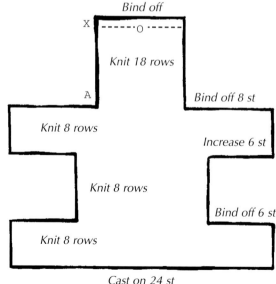

*Figure 82.
Pattern for a
knitted sheep.*

Bind off

X

Knit 18 rows

A

Bind off 8 st

Knit 8 rows

Increase 6 st

Knit 8 rows

Bind off 6 st

Knit 8 rows

Begin here   Cast on 24 st

Figure 83. Summer landscape.

Summertime

Two white horses on a green wool pasture, beside it a yellow field, and an indigo-blue carded roll as a river.

To make the tree, hang layers of different shades of green wool onto a twig, which is inserted into a lump of wax or clay.

Horse

❖ *3 pipe-cleaners*

c. 15 g (½ oz) white, long-stapled wool
Wrap a thin strand of wool firmly around one of the pipe-cleaners (head, neck and back). Bend as shown in the sketch (Figure 84). Bend both the other pipe-cleaners over the back and fix them crosswise with thin strands of wool. Then bend back the legs so they all have a length of about 3.5 cm (1½″) and wrap wool around them.

Wind a few thin layers of wool around the body to make it look like a horse. Make sure the neck is bent in an arch and gets thinner towards the head. If necessary use a thick needle to make the head and mouth.

Wind one or two layers of wool around the legs, getting fatter towards the body. If the strands of wool are wound firmly to the end they will not need sewing up. Lastly pull strands of wool through the body for the ears, mane and tail.

Autumn area

Make the meadow out of shades of green, yellow and orange and wind-swept, leaning trees. In the foreground a

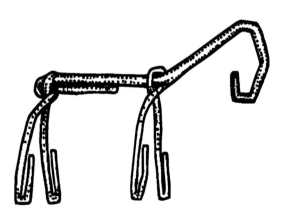

3 pipe cleaners, each 15 cm (6″) long.

Legs: 3.5 cm (1½″).

Back: 3.5 cm (1½″).

Head and neck: 5.5 cm (2″).

Figure 84. Horse (actual size)

Figure 85. Autumn landscape.

girl with flying plaits and blowing skirt and a child that is stretching his arms out towards the wind. See Pipe-cleaner Dolls, page 40.

Winter area

The landscape is made out of a big, white wool mat. Add a white ragged rock. The bare tree is inserted into a lump of wax or clay. The little snowman

Figure 86. Winter landscape.

adds a merry touch to the landscape. He is only 8 cm (3″) high, including hat. The three balls are made out of long-stapled, natural white wool; wind very firmly and sew together. The hat is made out of dark brown wool, felted between both hands with soap and water and sewn together. Eyes, mouth and buttons can be sewn on with thick yarn. Thread a long strand of wool through the body for the arms and the carrot nose.

Season's fairies

For the basic figure, see Basic Body, page 34. Making these elaborately decorated figures requires skill and patience.

Spring fairy

The colours of spring are pastel shades of pink, light blue, yellow, white and light green. For the tiny flowers use a card strip of 50 x 7 mm (2″ x ¼″). For instructions to make the flowers, see page 30.

   The cornucopia (horn of plenty) is felted. Wind some white wool around the card pattern (Figure 87), and wrap a

Figures 88 and 89. Spring fairy.

Figure 87. Pattern for the horn of plenty (actual size).

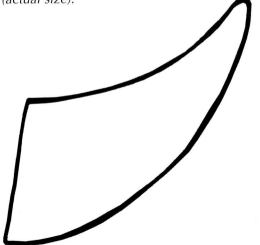

very thin golden strand around the outside. Dip it into hot water and rub it between soapy hands for about 15 minutes, carefully to begin with. Rub around the edges of the card repeatedly with forefinger and thumb to make sure the edges also get felted. Cut along the opening and remove the wet card.

For the scattered flowers, rub tiny fluffs of pink and white wool into balls between your fingertips. Tease pale green wool into a veil, the tiny flowers will get caught in it; bigger ones can be sewn on with a few stitches. Fasten the veil to the horn of plenty which is fixed to the arms of the doll. The flower veil should be long enough for it to be spread out on the ground and swirled around the hem of the skirt, which makes the fairy seem light and airy.

Summer fairy

In summer bright colours like light red, dark red, blue-violet, yellow and green are prominent. Lots of flowers adorn the dress and head band of the summer fairy (same size and method as for Spring fairy). The fairy appears to grow out of the flowers — with flowers sewn onto the hem of the skirt and felt leaves bent out-

Figures 90 and 91. Summer fairy.

wards. The stalk of the flower in her hand is a pipe-cleaner with green wool wound around it. The head-dress is also made out of a pipe-cleaner, formed into a circle with green wool wound round it and set with flowers. The green tendril in the head-dress is made by tightly winding a long strand of green wool around a pipe-cleaner, and unwinding it again after two to three days. This leaves it curly.

Autumn fairy

Warm colours like brown, yellow, red and orange adorn the autumn fairy. To make the sunflower takes a slightly wider card strip than the spring flowers. The brown flower centres are tufts of wool formed into a circle and sewn on. The apples are made by twisting some red and yellow wool between your fingertips, the pumpkin is wound like a doll's

Figures 92 and 93. Autumn fairy.

head. The pumpkin tendril and wavy hair is made as for the summer fairy.

The fairy in the picture is wearing earrings: dark blue baubles made out of tiny balls of wool twisted between fingertips.

Winter fairy

The dress of the winter fairy is white with some turquoise. It is surrounded by a white veil with snow flakes (made in the same way as the spring fairy's veil). The light blond hair is fastened into spirals over the ears. The ice crown is made out of clear gelatine. For the felted muff see the Figure 96; for instructions see the skirt of the moss-folk, page 52.

Figures 94 and 95. Winter-fairy.

Figure 96. Pattern wrapped with wool for the winter fairy's muff.

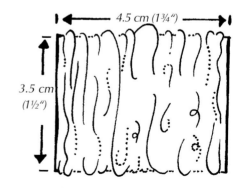

4.5 cm (1¾")

3.5 cm (1½")

Miniature pictures in a wooden frame

The wooden frames (11 x 8 cm, 4½″ x 3″) are made by hand. Make a small supply of them. The background is made of felt (see page 63 for how to make a felted mat), or use industrially made felt or a piece of rectangular card covered in silk. Staple the background onto the frame. The figures shown are all miniature

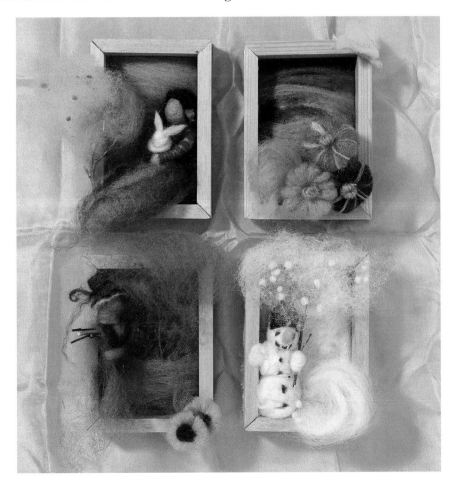

Figure 97. Miniature pictures with seasonal motifs.

copies of things described in this book, apart from the scarecrow, and are merely suggestions. The pictures appear more interesting if the motifs spill out of the frame a bit. These mini-pictures make an interesting present.

Figures 98 & 99. Plant dyed, carded fleeces.

A colourful nest

If the weather is nice we always tease and card the wool in the garden. One spring a pair of red-tailed birds were building a nest under the eaves. By autumn they had left their nest and we went to take a closer look. To our surprise we found the birds had picked up tufts of wool from the garden in spring and made a very colourful nest out of it!

Buying and Caring for Wool

Bought wool is usually washed and carded and ready for dyeing. Ask for long-stapled wool if you want to make figures mainly. Pure merino wool is nice and curly, but quite short staple. The wool from milk-sheep merino crossbreeds works very well. Hanks of wool, which have been carded and wound into thick balls, are usually long-stapled; mats and other pieces are usually short-stapled. Even if the wool is perfectly carded before being dyed, it still needs to be re-carded after dyeing. So you will need at least hand-carders if you want to dye wool yourself.

Mechanically-carded wool has often been stripped of its natural grease, making it feel lifeless and brittle. This effect is worse if the wool has been tightly packed for a long time. Rub lanolin into your hands before teasing the wool, it will spread into the wool and regenerate it. Carded wool and bought magic wool can also be treated in this fashion. After re-greasing, place the wool in the fresh air for a while; damp night air is ideal. You can feel the wool breathing in and coming to life.

Keep plant-dyed wool in a cool place. If you have dyed a larger reserve of wool, only card the amount you need just before using it. Do not keep wool tightly confined for any length of time; an old bed-cover is ideal for storing and protects against dust. Tomato leaves are good against moths, as are a few drops of lavender oil or cedar-wood shavings.

Magic Wool

Creative Activities with Natural Sheep's Wool

Dagmar Schmidt and Freya Jaffke

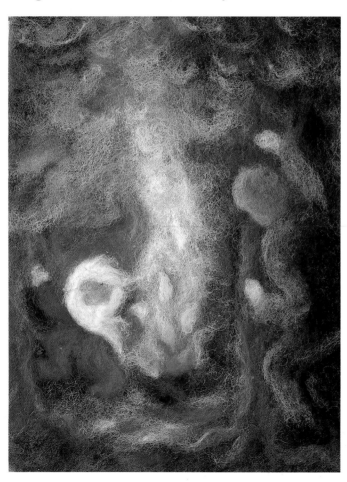

The authors combine their craft and teaching talents and experience to show how to create beautiful pictures, figures and animals using a variety of techniques.

Floris Books